PowerKiDS
Readers
AMERICAN SYMBOLS

THE FLAG

Joe Gaspar

PowerKiDS press.

New York

Published in 2014 by The Rosen Publishing Group, Inc.
29 East 21st Street, New York, NY 10010

First Edition

Editor: Amelie von Zumbusch
Book Design: Colleen Bialecki

Photo Credits: Cover Jamie Grill/Iconica/Getty Images; p. 5 Stockbyte/Thinkstock; p. 7 Andersen Ross/ Stockbyte/Getty Images; p. 9 Ron Sherman/Stone/Getty Images; p. 11 KidStock/Blend Images/Getty Images; p. 13 Dea Picture Library/Dea Agostini/Getty Images; p. 15 Ariel Skelley/Blend Images/Getty Images; p. 17 iStockphoto/Thinkstock; p. 19 Jupiter Images/Creatas/Thinkstock; p. 21 Jill Chen/Vetta/Getty Images; p. 23 AVAVA/Shutterstock.com.

Library of Congress Cataloging-in-Publication Data

Gaspar, Joe.
  The flag / by Joe Gaspar. — 1st ed.
      p. cm. — (Powerkids readers: American symbols)
  Includes index.
  ISBN 978-1-4777-0736-4 (library binding) — ISBN 978-1-4777-0813-2 (pbk.) —
  ISBN 978-1-4777-0814-9 (6-pack)
  1. Flags—United States—Juvenile literature. 2. Flag Day—Juvenile literature. I. Title.
  CR113.G37 2014
  929.9'20973—dc23
                                    2012043622

Manufactured in the United States of America

CPSIA Compliance Information: Batch #S13PK4: For Further Information contact Rosen Publishing, New York, New York at 1-800-237-9932

CONTENTS

This is our **flag**.

It is called Old Glory.

Some flags are big.

Some are small.

The first was made in 1777.

Each **star** stands for a state.

Hawaii was the fiftieth state.

The part with stars is the **union**.

Flag Day is June 14.

Do you have a flag?

WORDS TO KNOW

American flag

star

union

INDEX

WEBSITES

Due to the changing nature of Internet links, PowerKids Press has developed an online list of websites related to the subject of this book. This site is updated regularly. Please use this link to access the list: www.powerkidslinks.com/pkras/flag/